WARREN G.
HARDING

PRESIDENTIAL ✧ LEADERS

WARREN G. HARDING

ELAINE LANDAU

LERNER PUBLICATIONS COMPANY / MINNEAPOLIS

For Graham and Garrett Fulwood

Lerner Publications Company
A division of Lerner Publishing Group
241 First Avenue North
Minneapolis, MN 55401

Website address: www.lernerbooks.com

Library of Congress Cataloging-in-Publication Data

Landau, Elaine.
    Warren G. Harding / by Elaine Landau.
        p.   cm. — (Presidential leaders)
    Includes bibliographical references and index.
    ISBN: 0–8225–0850–8 (lib. bdg. : alk. paper)
    1. Harding, Warren G. (Warren Gamaliel), 1865–1923—Juvenile literature.
    2. Presidents—United States—Biography—Juvenile literature. [1. Harding, Warren G.
    (Warren Gamaliel), 1865–1923. 2. Presidents.] I. Title. II. Series.
    E786.L36 2005
    973.91'4'092—dc22   2003026410

Manufactured in the United States of America
1 2 3 4 5 6 – JR – 10 09 08 07 06 05

G. Harding (**center**) *began his term as the twenty-ninth president*
he United States in 1921 with a confident and optimistic speech.

CONTENTS

———— ✧ ————

*Warr
of*

INTRODUCTION

I am a man of limited talents from a small
town. I don't seem to grasp that I am president.
—Warren G. Harding

March 4, 1921, was an exciting day in Washington, D.C., the nation's capital. Warren G. Harding was about to be sworn in as president of the United States. Capitol Park, across from the East Portico of the Capitol Building, overflowed with people eager to witness the inaugural ceremony. Young boys had climbed trees to sneak a peek at the new national leader. Fifty soldiers who had been injured in World War I (1914–1918) were brought in for the occasion in wheelchairs.

Less than a year earlier, Harding had been a largely unknown politician. But in the 1920 election, he received the greatest number of votes of any presidential candidate in more than a century. People in the United States were ready for a rest from wartime troubles. Americans looked to their new president to bring back the carefree days they had once enjoyed. With a campaign that promised a "return to normalcy," Harding was swept into office by an overwhelming 60 percent of the popular vote.

At the inaugural ceremony, the stately, good-looking president-elect stood next to outgoing president Woodrow Wilson. As Harding prepared to take the oath of office, he placed his left hand on the Bible and raised his right hand. In a deep, resounding voice, he repeated the words:

"I, Warren Gamaliel Harding, do solemnly swear that I will faithfully execute the office of the President of the United States and will, to the best of my ability, preserve, protect, and defend the Constitution of the United States, so help me God."

Harding spoke with determination and confidence. Since this was the first presidential swearing-in ceremony in which a microphone was used, his words were heard for blocks. Applause filled the air when he finished. People stood to honor him, while some in the crowd cried for joy. Yet the new president simply turned to a senator who stood beside him and whispered, "Was it done all right?" Those who knew Harding probably would not have been surprised at his question. Harding often relied on friends and associates for feedback on important issues.

In his inaugural speech, Harding promised better times. World War I had recently ended. Known as the war to end all wars, the conflict had involved the United States as well as Europe's great powers. During the war, which began in 1914, Germany, Austria-Hungary, Turkey, and other nations had formed an alliance known as the Central powers. The Central powers fought against the Allies, a group that included Great Britain, France, Russia, Italy, Portugal, Belgium, Japan and, beginning in 1917, the United States.

American troops celebrated the end of World War I, but they faced difficult times when they returned home.

✧

The Allies won, but the cost was great to both sides. By the time the war was over, in November 1918, about ten million soldiers had died and nearly twice that number were wounded.

Harding's words inspired hope, but who was this new president? Would he be able to deliver what he said?

CHAPTER ONE

HUMBLE BEGINNINGS

Winnie [Warren] is bright beyond his years.
—Warren G. Harding's mother
describing him as a toddler

Warren Gamaliel Harding was born on November 2, 1865, in a white clapboard house in the small farming community of Blooming Grove, Ohio. Harding was the first president to be born after the Civil War (1861–1865) and the seventh president to be born in Ohio.

Warren's parents were used to being around babies. Both came from big families and worked in the medical profession. Warren's father, George Tryon Harding (known as Tryon), was a doctor. His mother, Phoebe Dickerson Harding, was a midwife, delivering babies for local women. Neither had dreamed of a career in medicine. Tryon was a teacher before he decided to study medicine, and Phoebe took up midwifery to supplement her husband's frequently unpredictable income.

Harding was born in this farmhouse in Blooming Grove, Ohio.

─────────────────── ✧ ───────────────────

Tryon came from one of the oldest and most respected families in Blooming Grove. The Hardings claimed to have descended from the Pilgrims at Plymouth Rock. For a time, Blooming Grove had even been called Harding Corners.

But Tryon wasn't as ambitious as most of the people in his family. As a physician, he never built up much of a practice. He reportedly spent most afternoons napping on his office couch. Tryon had seemed happiest when he had worked as a horse trader, and many people who knew him felt that "swapping" was his true passion. Throughout his life, he was involved in various swaps, trades, and deals. He would trade just about anything he had for cattle, farm tools, or a piece of machinery that caught his eye. Some of these swaps were more successful than others. At times, Tryon was financially ahead, but often his family had to bail him out.

George Tryon Harding

——————— ✧ ———————

Warren's mother, on the other hand, was both practical and deeply religious. A Methodist, Phoebe went to church every day and insisted that her family accompany her on Sundays. She often hummed religious hymns, and much of the advice she gave came in the form of Bible quotations.

Phoebe was a pretty woman with kind eyes and a warm smile. She was also an extremely hard worker and devoted mother. Her days were filled with cooking, cleaning, baking, and caring for her children, in addition to her work helping local women deliver their babies.

PHOEBE AND WARREN

Warren was the oldest of eight children in his family. Although Phoebe loved all her children, she felt especially close to Warren. She had a special bond with her firstborn. Phoebe believed that Warren, whom she called Winnie, could be anything he wanted—even president of the United States.

Warren's mother did all she could to help her son achieve his potential. She tried to advance his education. Despite her many duties, Phoebe took time every day to read to the boy. She made sure that Warren knew the alphabet before he was four years old. She also taught him many poems, which he proudly recited for relatives and family friends. The young boy reveled in their praise.

Phoebe Dickerson Harding

——————— ✧ ———————

LIFE IN BLOOMING GROVE

Growing up in a rural farming community, Warren and his friends spent the summers fishing and swimming. Sometimes the boys played baseball into the early evening. During the fall, they went out to gather hickory nuts and butternuts for their families to enjoy. Often the boys tagged along with groups of local men who hunted geese, squirrels, quails, and turkeys. Warren liked sports and enjoyed being outdoors with his friends.

His mother, however, placed more emphasis on education. She made sure that Warren did not miss school and that he spent enough time studying. Warren attended a one-room schoolhouse that his grandfather had built for the area's children. Inside the school, boys and girls sat separately in rows of desks. Outside stood an outhouse and a woodshed.

Warren attended the village school for several years. He learned the basics in reading, writing, and arithmetic, as well as some history and geography. The coaching in recitation that he had received from his mother paid off. Early on, his teacher noticed the boy's excellent speaking ability.

THE UNSETTLING RUMOR

Sometimes, however, going to school or even just being around other children turned into an unpleasant experience for Warren. Other children called him names, using racial slurs. Their taunts stemmed from a rumor that had circulated around town for years—that the Hardings had an African American somewhere in the family tree. The rumor was fueled by the fact that Warren and some of his siblings had dark eyes and hair and olive skin. Some people in Blooming Grove said that Warren's great-grandfather had come from the West Indies. Others felt certain that another family member was African American.

No one ever knew for certain whether the rumor was true. Yet the truth didn't really matter. Warren was regarded as nonwhite at a time when racial prejudice was the norm. In the post-Civil War era, African Americans still faced the legacy and stigma of slavery on a daily basis. People of color had few rights they could count on. Whites and blacks largely led separate lives in what sometimes seemed like separate worlds.

Warren, his brothers and sisters, his cousins, and even his young aunts and uncles had to deal with the racial taunts. Some of the Harding children fought back. Punches flew and one or more of the youngsters came home with a black eye or a bloody nose.

But Warren took a different approach. More than anything else, he wanted to belong. Warren reacted to the slurs by trying harder than ever to fit in and be popular. He worked on making himself so agreeable that no one would exclude him. He learned how to please and get along well with those around him and how to be a good friend. He made a point of never losing his temper and took pride in being a good sport.

As a result, Warren became well liked. But he paid a price for this acceptance. Pressured by the need to please other people and conform to their views, Warren never developed a firm sense of self-confidence or decisiveness. Throughout much of his life, he was haunted by self-doubts and depended heavily on the advice and support of others.

CHAPTER TWO

WORK AND POLITICS

He was one of us, and he insisted that we worked "with him" not "for him."
—Jack Warwick, childhood friend and later an employee of Warren G. Harding

Warren did not complete his education in Blooming Grove. In 1873, when Warren was almost eight, his father moved the family to the nearby town of Caledonia. Though still a small town, Caledonia had several churches, a two-story school, and nearly seven hundred residents.

In many ways, Warren's life went on much as it had in Blooming Grove. The family's new house was close to the Methodist church, and Warren and his brothers and sisters attended frequently.

Warren enrolled in Caledonia's school, where he continued to do well. His teachers found him intelligent, but Warren did not show off in school, and sometimes he even downplayed his abilities. He made new friends, which gave

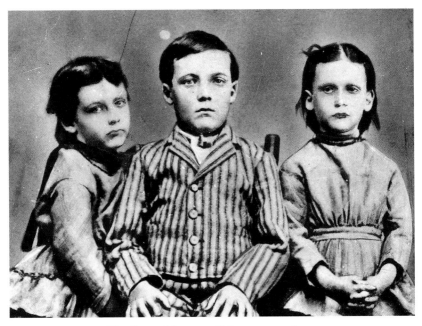

Harding with two of his younger sisters

him an effective buffer against any teasers. He also partici-
pated in extracurricular activities. He often took part in the
school's Friday afternoon declamation (recitation) contests.
Having practiced for years in front of his mother and other
family members, he usually did strikingly well.

While Warren liked reciting, perhaps his fondest childhood pastime began in 1875, when he was ten. That was
when his father brought home a cornet, a brass instrument similar to a trumpet, for Warren. The cornet was
not new. It was a used one that his father had acquired in
one of his trades. Nevertheless, Warren cherished the
instrument and kept his younger brothers and sisters from
playing with it.

Warren began taking cornet lessons and learned quickly. It wasn't long before he was good enough to join the Caledonia Aeolian Band. The local band played in the town's bandstand on Saturday nights and sometimes entertained in nearby towns and villages. Harding put his heart and soul into his music. As one of his friends said, "He could execute No. 24 in the Black Book with . . . astonishing musical force. Barring the bass drummer, no other member of the band could make as much noise."

FIRST JOB

The year 1875 was important to Warren for another reason besides getting a cornet. As the result of yet another trade, his father gained ownership of the *Caledonia Argus,* the town newspaper. Warren, along with another boy, worked for free at the paper after school. The boys ran errands and cleaned up. But they also had a chance to learn about typesetting and other aspects of the printing business.

At the time, most young boys worked on their family's or a neighbor's farm. Early on, however, it was clear that Warren preferred using his mind to doing farmwork. According to one story, when Warren was twelve years old, he was paid fifty cents a day by a nearby farmer to shuck corn husks. Warren quit after the first day, complaining that the work was too hard. He told his father that he would rather spend his spare time working at the *Caledonia Argus,* even though he wasn't paid for it. He taught his little sister to milk the family's cow and do other chores so that he could be at the newspaper more often.

That wasn't always possible. Sometimes his family needed money badly. When Harding was a young teen, his

*Milking the cows was a chore frequently assigned
to the children in a farm family.*

─────────────── ✧ ───────────────

parents often asked him to find outside work to help with
the family finances. Warren painted barns and "grained"
wood. By learning to artfully mix and apply various paints
and stains, Warren was able to turn a plain pinewood board
into a fine-looking imitation of cherry or mahogany wood.
But this work didn't bring in enough money to support the
large family.

By 1879 Tryon Harding's various business ventures had
reached a new low. While he still worked as a doctor, he
did not earn very much money. Often his patients could
not afford to pay him in cash. Instead, they'd bring him
eggs and butter from their farms. Tryon and his family, no
longer able to afford their Caledonia home, were forced
to move to a small farm in the next county. More than
ever before, the Hardings depended on Phoebe's earnings

as a midwife. Despite the family's lack of financial resources, Warren managed to enter Iberia College (later renamed Ohio Central College) in nearby Iberia, Ohio. He was just fourteen at the time.

COLLEGE AND BEYOND

The Iberia College faculty was small, with just two pastors and a Latin professor. The student body was comparably tiny. Warren's graduating class had just two students. One of his friends later joked that Warren graduated either "first or second in his class." While at the school, Warren used his background in the newspaper business to start a student newspaper. Called the *Iberia Spectator,* the four-page publication contained local news, editorials, and jokes. Six issues were published, but when Warren graduated in 1882, the paper came to an end.

Following his graduation, Warren didn't immediately settle on a career. By then his father had again moved the family. The Hardings were living in Marion, the county seat of Marion County, Ohio. Warren returned home after college and looked for work in Marion. He taught school for a short time and sold insurance. He also toyed with the idea of becoming an attorney but decided against it.

Warren continued to be skilled at winning people over, and he soon became a popular figure in Marion. He cultivated numerous friendships as he spent hours at the horse stable or courthouse discussing politics. Sometimes it seemed that he could go on for hours with these lengthy conversations, which he referred to as "bloviating."

BECOMING A NEWSPAPERMAN

Eventually, Harding found himself drawn into the newspaper business, again thanks to his father. In 1884 Tryon acquired half ownership of the *Marion Star* newspaper, and Warren served as an editor. Due to poor financial dealings, however, his father lost his share of the newspaper later that year. Warren, along with two boyhood friends, managed to buy back the publication. In time Harding bought out his two partners and became the *Star's* sole owner.

Harding's newspaper presented an extremely positive view of Marion. In an attempt to avoid scandalous stories,

———————————— ◇ ————————————

The offices of the Marion Star *in Marion, Ohio*

Harding at the age of twenty-one
——————— ✧ ———————

Harding played down incidents involving Marion residents "whose weaknesses got them into trouble." He once told a newspaper associate that he wished "we could cut out all police court news." Instead, the *Marion Star* served as a community booster, faithfully covering new business openings, town celebrations, and cultural events.

THE REPUBLICAN

Following his father's lead, Harding joined the Republican Party in the late 1880s. Warren enjoyed participating in the local Young Men's Republican Club. After purchasing the *Marion Star,* Harding announced that the publication would reflect Republican values, such as strong support for businesses in Marion. Many business owners were also Republicans, and a firm bond developed between them and Harding. This benefited Harding personally as well as professionally. As the town grew and prospered, so did the *Star* and its owner.

It wasn't long before Harding was regarded as a loyal Republican. On several occasions, he served as a delegate to the Republican state convention, where party members nominated candidates for state and national elections.

The *Marion Star* Creed

Harding's attitude is reflected in the creed, or set of principles, that he wrote for his newspaper staff.

The *Star* Office Creed
- Remember there are two sides to every question. Get both.
- Be truthful.
- Get the facts. Mistakes are inevitable, but strive for accuracy. I would rather have one story exactly right than a hundred half wrong.
- Be decent. Be fair. Be generous.
- Boost—don't knock. There's good in everybody. Bring out the good in everybody, and never needlessly hurt the feelings of anybody.
- In reporting a political gathering, get the facts; tell the story as it is, not as you would like to have it.
- Treat all parties alike. If there's any politics to be played, we will play it in our editorial columns.
- Treat all religious matters reverently.
- If it can possibly be avoided, never bring ignominy [disgrace or dishonor] to an innocent woman or child in telling of the misdeeds or misfortune of a relative.
- Don't wait to be asked, but do it without asking.
- And, above all, be clean. Never let a dirty word or suggestive story get into type.
  I want this paper so conducted that it can go into any home without destroying the innocence of any child.

—Warren G. Harding, Editor & Publisher of the *Marion Star*

Harding entered Battle Creek Sanitarium for the first time in 1889. The health center's director was John Harvey Kellogg, the inventor of cornflakes.

⟡

In both his work and politics, Harding continuously strove to succeed. The constant pressure of trying to please people and overcome his own self-doubts and insecurities proved stressful. In October 1889, he suffered a mental collapse, which he called a nervous breakdown. On October 16, the *Star* noted that Mr. Harding was "indisposed to such an extent that he is unable to attend to any newspaper duties, being scarcely able to reach the office for half an hour each day."

At his father's urging, the twenty-four-year-old Harding spent several weeks at the Battle Creek Sanitarium in Battle Creek, Michigan. The sanitarium was a health and fitness retreat run by Dr. John Harvey Kellogg, the man who had invented cornflakes. Harding's stay at Battle Creek seemed to do wonders for him. He returned to Marion rested and fit. He was again able to enjoy his newspaper, his friends, and his political activities.

ENTER FLORENCE KLING
Harding enjoyed the attention of many young women in Marion. He had grown into a strikingly handsome young man, and there was no shortage of women eager to spend time with him. Once Florence Mabel Kling set her sights on Harding, however, few other women had a chance.

Florence Kling was five years older than Warren. She was the daughter of Amos Kling, a successful

Florence Mabel Kling
——— ✧ ———

real estate developer who was one of the wealthiest men in Marion. Through the years, Florence's relationship with her father had been stormy. Amos had always wished that his firstborn child had been a boy instead of a girl.

As intelligent as her father, Florence, nicknamed Flossie, was also just as determined and stubborn. Though she was considered rather plain, she had a keen mind and sharp wit. A close friend of the family once described Florence as a child: "She did not take life as she found it. She grasped it fearlessly and firmly and forced it to yield to her demands."

In 1880 Florence had embarked on her first marriage. She eloped with Pete De Wolfe, a neighbor's son. Although Pete came from a highly respected family, he had few goals. After the marriage, he mostly rested during the day and spent his nights drinking. The couple had a son, Marshall, but Pete took almost no interest in him. As the boy grew older, Florence's interest in him also waned. When she and Pete divorced in 1886, Marshall went to live with his grandparents.

Proud and independent, Florence refused to return to her father's house after her divorce. In the late 1800s, it was unusual for a woman not only to get divorced but also to live alone. In those days, women were expected to live either with their parents or their husbands, and few were encouraged to support themselves financially. But Florence was determined to run her own life. She earned money by renting out rooms in her house and giving piano lessons.

Among her students was one of Warren Harding's younger sisters, Charity. Florence had noticed Charity's tall, handsome brother around town even before the girl started taking lessons. One day, Warren happened to walk into the parlor at his parent's home while Florence was working at the piano with his little sister. At the time, Warren was twenty-five and Florence was thirty. Flossie was immediately taken with Warren. She made every effort to see him whenever possible.

COURTSHIP AND MARRIAGE

At first, Harding did not return Florence's feelings, but over time he warmed up to her. Dating a woman of her background was a step up for him socially, and he was

Florence taught piano lessons on a piano that may have looked something like this one from the late 1800s.

——————————— ✧ ———————————

interested in advancing his career. Harding also liked Florence's perseverance and determination, qualities that he sometimes wished were stronger in him.

As the months passed, people began to think of the two as a couple, and Harding gave in to the idea. But being Florence's beau was not easy. She was extremely possessive and continually kept track of his whereabouts. Sometimes Harding tried to sneak off and take the train to Caledonia to see an old girlfriend. More often than not, Florence would guess where he was and be waiting at the train station when he returned. One time he saw her from the train window and tried to avoid her by exiting the train car from the opposite side. But he didn't get past her. Florence loudly called out to him, "You needn't try to run away, Warren Harding. I can see your big feet."

The couple eventually decided to marry. Some observers said that Florence's domineering nature simply wore down Harding's resistance. But others felt there was more to it than that. Harding may not have been as passive about the relationship as he appeared to be. The *Marion Star* needed a financial boost. Marrying into the richest and most prestigious family in town could help Harding in his political life.

Yet Harding was mistaken if he thought he could easily join the Kling family. Amos Kling was adamantly opposed to the relationship. He had heard the rumors about Harding's mixed racial background and was furious at the thought of his daughter marrying him. One day when Amos passed Harding on the street, Amos flew into a rage and began screaming racial slurs at the young man. Kling warned Harding that if he continued seeing his daughter, he would blow Harding's head off.

Amos Kling never went as far as murder. But he tried to make things as uncomfortable as possible for the entire Harding family. He bought up all of Tryon Harding's gambling debts. Knowing that Tryon could not afford to repay the debts immediately, Kling brought several lawsuits against him demanding payment. Kling also found ways to use his influence and wealth to harm Warren Harding. He discouraged his friends from advertising in the *Marion Star*. Years later, Kling even started a rival newspaper to try to drive Harding out of business.

Kling turned his anger on his daughter as well. When he saw her in town, he refused to acknowledge her. He insisted that his wife have nothing to do with their daughter either. None of this deterred Florence, who knew her own mind and was easily a match for her father.

With the support of Warren's family behind them, Florence and Warren planned their own wedding. It was held on July 8, 1891, in a house in Marion that the couple had built for themselves. More than one hundred people

———————————— ✧ ————————————

The Hardings' home in Marion, Ohio

attended the ceremony—but Florence's father was not among them. When he learned that one of his close friends had gone to the wedding, he was furious. The next time he saw the man, he cursed him and swore that their friendship was over.

Harding's father-in-law was not a man who easily reconciled. Amos Kling had nothing to do with his daughter and son-in-law for the next fifteen years.

CHAPTER THREE

PUBLIC LIFE, PRIVATE LIFE

I have only one real hobby—my husband.
—Florence Harding

In marrying Florence, Warren Harding may not have gained access to her family's fortune, but he did gain the support of a strong, ambitious woman. Florence Harding loved her husband and believed that he had a promising future. She wanted Warren to be respected, wealthy, and successful. Florence was always coming up with ways her husband could advance. She intended to be the driving force behind him, and her energy to help him seemed boundless.

Some historians believe that Florence was too over-powering for her husband. Others think that Harding had some difficulty adjusting to married life. In any case, shortly after the wedding, he began to suffer regularly from painful bouts of indigestion. These episodes were so severe that at times he was barely able to stand. During the first weeks of his marriage, Harding was often in excruciating pain. Many nights he needed medical help and had to send for his father.

Harding's indigestion became so frequent that Tryon Harding persuaded the newlyweds to move in with the Harding family. That way, Tryon would always be available to treat his son. The young couple agreed, and they lived with Warren's parents for nearly six months. Though Harding was able to get help when he needed it, the arrangement had some drawbacks. Feelings were often tense in the crowded household. Florence never liked being there and was greatly relieved when Warren was well enough to go home.

ON THE ROAD

Florence's husband did not remain at home for very long, however. Using the free railroad passes he received to cover news events, Harding spent a good deal of time traveling. He was restless, and travel seemed to free his spirit. Sometimes his trips had a definite purpose. Harding traveled throughout Ohio for various Republican Party functions. At these meetings, he often gave rousing speeches. People in the audience commented on Harding's good looks and wonderful voice.

Everywhere he went, Harding made a point of making friends. He loved getting to know new people, and political functions gave him the opportunity to do so. In 1892 Harding made his first trip to Washington, D.C., where he met with Ohio senators and congressional representatives. As he expanded his political network, Harding enhanced his image and his own potential within the Republican Party.

*Harding's trip to Washington, D.C., in 1892
helped advance his political career.*

❖

These maneuvers also had the benefit of giving Harding a legitimate reason to be away from home for long periods. During the early years of his marriage, he usually traveled alone and liked it that way. Despite his absences, Florence remained devoted to her husband. Although Harding wasn't in love with his wife, he admired her and relied on her to keep their lives on track.

BACK TO BATTLE CREEK

Beneath the polished exterior Harding presented to the world, he often felt troubled. He had difficulty coping with stress and suffered from feelings of inadequacy. By early 1894, he was on the verge of a second mental breakdown.

On January 7, 1894, he returned to the Battle Creek Sanitarium, where he remained until almost the end of February. His "rest cure" consisted of relaxation and wholesome food. Harding improved somewhat, but he was back home for only about two months before he returned to the sanitarium. This time he stayed at Battle Creek until the fall.

While Harding was at the sanitarium, the *Marion Star*'s business manager left the paper. Florence, who had always had good business sense, took over the job. Riding her

bicycle to the newspaper office each day, Florence immediately set about reorganizing a number of office procedures. She also started home delivery of newspapers in Marion. The changes she made improved overall efficiency and increased profits.

✧ ————————
Harding in his office at the Marion Star

After returning from Battle Creek, Harding resumed his role as newspaper publisher and worked on several Republican Party committees. In January 1895, he began to feel on edge again, but this time, he chose not to return to the sanitarium. Instead, he and Florence went on an extended vacation to Florida. Although Florida was a bit chilly that winter, it was still a welcome change from the freezing Ohio winter.

The vacation proved to be just what Harding needed. Life had become extremely difficult for him in Marion. Stinging editorial attacks from rival newspapers had become quite personal. The *Dollar Democrat,* a weekly Democratic newspaper, revived the old stories about Harding's African American background. In one issue, the paper printed a silhouette of Harding, stating that the figure's features could not be filled in because of its dark color. By playing on racial tensions, the newspaper hoped to hurt both the *Star* and Harding's political aspirations.

It accomplished neither goal, however. The *Star* thrived, and Harding returned from Florida in time to play an active part in the April 1895 Marion County Republican Convention. Harding's work for the party helped him become better known in Marion and the surrounding region. Newspapers throughout the state began to applaud Harding as "a faithful and untiring Republican worker."

FIRST ELECTED OFFICE

In the late 1800s, Ohio's Republican Party was split into many factions (groups) that were constantly battling for power. Corruption and conflicts of interest were common in many parts of the state, and people's political loyalties were continually shifting. Powerful party leaders, or "bosses" as they were called, might be allies one day and enemies the next. In most cases, these leaders were less concerned about important issues and ideas than they were about holding on to control of the party and keeping the money they felt was coming to them.

Harding avoided taking sides and did his best to get along well with all the groups. He encouraged his fellow Republicans to put aside their differences so they could continue to defeat the Democrats. He called his approach "harmonizing."

Yet Harding wasn't thinking just of the party. He wanted to advance his own political career as well. After years of serving the Republican Party, he realized that if he weren't elected to public office soon, it might never happen. So he let it be known that he wanted to be the Republican candidate from his district in the Ohio State Senate election of 1898. The reaction was favorable. One Ohio paper described Harding as "a congenial [friendly] fellow" and added that "the Republicans could not select a better man." Harding easily won both the Republican nomination and the election that fall.

In his first elected office, Harding took a middle-of-the-road approach. He believed in high tariffs, or taxes on imported foreign goods, as a way to protect U.S. businesses from competition from foreign companies. Like many Republicans of his day, Harding tended to distrust labor unions (groups of workers organized to demand better wages and working conditions). Yet he believed in providing a decent wage for U.S. workers.

Harding also favored limits on immigration, because he feared that large numbers of immigrants would create an oversupply of laborers and lead to lower wages for all workers. He went back and forth on the question of Prohibition, a ban on the manufacture and sale of alcoholic beverages. While Harding enjoyed a drink himself, he knew that support for a "dry" Ohio was on the rise.

As he had in the past, Harding avoided taking sides in party disputes and granted favors equally to Republican legislators from various parts of the state. He soon established a reputation as a savvy deal maker. As the state's governor noted at the time, "There may be an abler man in the Senate than Harding but when I want things done I go to him."

Harding knew he would never be a party boss—one of the leaders who had firm control over the party. Harding lacked the ruthless desire for power necessary to achieve that goal. Instead, he saw his role as a conciliator (peacemaker) who relied on "harmonizing" to get past roadblocks. As one Republican Party observer noted, "In the Ohio Senate, Harding proved a great harmonizer. He had the unusual gift of getting people together and inducing them to patch up differences."

Harding hadn't abandoned his political ambitions, however. He still hoped to rise within the party. Florence was also anxious to see him move up. Harding had begun calling his wife "the Duchess." Although he had not chosen the nickname as a compliment, it stuck. The Duchess felt that her husband had not yet reached his true potential. She continually urged him to set higher goals for himself.

THE NOBLE EXPERIMENT

The Eighteenth Amendment to the U.S. Constitution was ratified (approved) in 1919, and Prohibition became the law of the land. The outlawing of the manufacture and sale of alcoholic beverages lasted from 1920 to 1933 and is sometimes referred to as the "noble experiment." It was an experiment that failed badly.

Supporters of Prohibition believed that outlawing liquor would bring an end to many social ills. They hoped it would reduce unemployment, divorce, and crime. Yet Prohibition accomplished none of these things. Although drinking levels decreased at first, people in the United States actually ended up drinking more alcohol during Prohibition than before the law was passed.

This was largely due to the illegal production and import of alcoholic beverages. Illegal drinking establishments, known as speakeasies, opened throughout the country. Unlike saloons, speakeasies were not subject to local laws that limited their hours and days of operation. The small, hidden bars were always busy and never seemed to close.

Prohibition enthusiasts expected that people would put the money they had previously spent on alcohol into education, life insurance, savings accounts, and other beneficial measures. This didn't happen either. During Prohibition, people spent more money on alcohol than ever before. Spending on alcohol substitutes also skyrocketed. These included narcotics, hashish, tobacco, and marijuana.

MOVING UP THE PARTY LADDER

By 1904 some Ohio Republicans thought that Harding might be a good candidate for governor. The party bosses, however, favored a man named Myron T. Herrick. Ever the loyal party member, Harding graciously backed off. Yet he managed to get a place for himself on the ticket as lieutenant governor, the second in command in the state. The team of Herrick and Harding won the election. As lieutenant governor, Harding spent much of his time making speeches throughout the state and broadening his circle of support.

Herrick was up for reelection in 1906, but his chances of winning didn't look good. In just a short time, the governor had alienated a number of key special interest groups, such as supporters of Prohibition. Harding, on the other hand, had managed to stay in most people's good graces. He knew that Herrick wanted to run for reelection. But he also knew that if

———————— ✧
Myron T. Herrick (right) served as governor of Ohio with Harding as his lieutenant governor.

Herrick ran, he was sure to lose. Harding told party leaders that he wanted to replace Herrick as the Republican gubernatorial candidate.

Some influential party members thought Harding was stepping out of line, and they refused to back him for governor. Herrick ran again, but this time around, Harding declined to run as lieutenant governor. He didn't want to be part of a losing duo. As he expected, Herrick's reelection bid was unsuccessful.

Harding returned full-time to his job at the *Marion Star*. In the future, he would think twice about bucking the party bosses. Meanwhile, the time he had spent as lieutenant governor had greatly enhanced his status in Marion.

Harding (left) *works on typesetting at the* Marion Star. *At the time, newspaper type was all set in place by hand.*

He was considered a leading town citizen. He and Florence were invited to social events hosted by the wealthiest and most influential Marion residents. Even Harding's father-in-law, Amos Kling, began to warm up to him.

ANOTHER WOMAN

Among the Hardings' friends was a couple named Jim and Carrie Phillips. Jim Phillips was the co-owner of a general store in town. When Jim became ill in 1905, Harding suggested that he spend some time at the Battle Creek Sanitarium. At the same time, Florence was away while recovering from surgery for a kidney aliment. Harding continued to visit with Carrie while their spouses were gone. Soon the relationship took a romantic turn.

Harding had not always been faithful to the Duchess. It is likely that Florence was aware of his extramarital affairs and chose to ignore them. Whenever possible, though, she tried to limit Warren's contact with other women. She often accompanied him to events and functions if she thought pretty young girls might be present.

Florence probably did not expect that her husband would become involved with any of their close friends. So when he fell in love with a woman from their own social circle, at first, Florence did not suspect anything.

Carrie Phillips proved to be more than just a passing fancy for Harding. He adored her, and their affair lasted for several years. In numerous letters to her, Harding praised Carrie's beauty and expressed his desire for her. The couple met secretly whenever they could. Sometimes Carrie joined Harding in another part of the state when he traveled to make a speech for the Republican Party. Amazingly, during this period, the Hardings and the Phillips still went out together socially. The two couples even took a month-long European vacation.

In 1910 Harding, then forty-four years old, tried to take another step forward in politics. After winning the Republican Party's nomination for governor, he ran against Ohio's Democratic governor Judson Harmon. Harmon was known for his exposure of corruption among a number of former Republican officials. Harding campaigned hard, making more than three hundred speeches throughout rural Ohio. But to his disappointment, he lost the election. Harding also endured another loss that year. In late May, his mother Phoebe died after being bedridden for several months following a serious fall.

Carrie didn't seem to care about the lost governorship or Phoebe's death. She offered little consolation to Harding when he needed it most. He finally broke off their relationship. Although it's not clear why he stopped seeing her, it may have had something to do with his political agenda. The Duchess was firmly committed to helping him achieve his political aims. Carrie, however, was one of the few people in Harding's life who encouraged him to leave politics. His political career took time away from her, and Carrie felt that she had already had to share him with others for too long.

Carrie went with her daughter to live in Europe for a time. When she returned, she came home to her husband. Meanwhile, Harding stayed married to the Duchess and played by the Republican Party rules.

CHAPTER FOUR

THE PARTY'S MAN

We must have a citizenship less concerned about what the government can do for it and more anxious about what it can do for the nation.
—Warren G. Harding

By 1912 trouble was brewing in the Republican Party. The Old Guard of the party—the conservative, traditional wing—was under attack from a growing reform movement within the party. The Progressive movement, as it was called, was led by Theodore Roosevelt, a former U.S. president and an outspoken Republican. The party bosses feared Roosevelt and his followers. The bosses knew that if the Progressive cause gained momentum, the Old Guard could lose control of the party. They were prepared to do whatever was necessary to stop the Progressives.

The conflict came to a head during the presidential election that year. The president at the time was Republican William Howard Taft, who had been the Old Guard's choice.

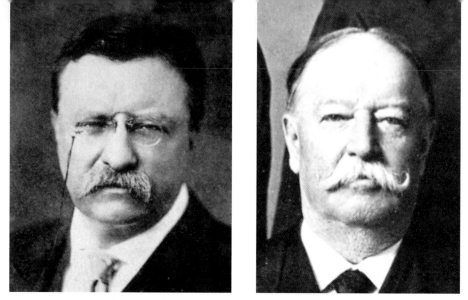

In 1912 the Republican Party was split between former president Theodore Roosevelt (left), who led the Progressives, and President William H. Taft (right), who stayed with the Old Guard.

Although Taft's chances for reelection looked doubtful, he agreed to run for a second term for the benefit of the party. The Progressives wanted former president Roosevelt to run instead of Taft, but the Old Guard bosses blocked their efforts. They had no intention of giving up control of the party, even if it meant losing the presidency to the Democrats.

A KEY SPEECH

Harding remained faithful to the Old Guard of the party. In return for his loyalty, he was selected to give the presidential nominating speech for Taft at the 1912 Republican National Convention in Chicago that June. Even though Harding had been making political speeches for years, this one was more difficult than any other he had given. The moment he stepped up to the podium, he became a symbol of the Old Guard. To the Progressives, he represented the party bosses' efforts to push through Taft's nomination. Jeers and hisses sounded as Harding began speaking, and the catcalls didn't stop. Some people even walked out in protest.

Through it all, Harding stood gallantly at the podium. Dressed in a new, long-tailed jacket with a deep red flower in his lapel, he looked handsome and sophisticated. His voice had its usual luster, but this mattered little to the reformers in the audience. To them Harding seemed like a party hack pushing through a preplanned agenda.

——————————— ✧ ———————————

Although Harding preferred to compromise rather than choose sides, he aligned himself with the Old Guard at the Republican Convention of 1912 (below).

THE OLD GUARD VS. THE PROGRESSIVES

By 1912 a serious divide had formed within the Republican Party. The Old Guard had been in power for years and favored traditional Republican policies, such as high tariffs and other protections for U.S. businesses. The Old Guard was being challenged by the Progressives, who wanted their party to accept many new reforms, including a national tariff reduction, child labor laws, old-age pensions, women's suffrage (right to vote), environmental conservation, and minimum wage laws.

The leader of the Progressives was Theodore Roosevelt, who had served as U.S. president from 1901 to 1909. In 1912 Roosevelt decided to run for a third term, and he wanted the Republican Party to nominate him as its candidate. But the Old Guard continued to support William Howard Taft, the current Republican president who supported the Old Guard's views.

Enraged, Roosevelt and his Progressive supporters left the Republican Party and formed their own third party, known as the Progressive Party, or Bull Moose Party. Roosevelt was the new party's presidential candidate in 1912. Although he lost the election, he still received more votes than Taft. As a result of the split within the Republican Party, Democratic candidate Woodrow Wilson won the election that year.

As it turned out, the Progressive Party was quite short-lived. In 1916 Roosevelt turned down the party's nomination to run as its presidential candidate. Instead, he and many of his followers returned to the Republican Party. What was left of the Progressive Party soon folded.

During the vote, the Old Guard held on to its power and Taft received the party's presidential nomination. As many Republicans had expected, Taft lost the election to Democrat Woodrow Wilson. The Progressives were angry but were not about to give up. The Old Guard remained determined to nominate only candidates whose loyalty was assured.

ON TO THE SENATE

One person who was known to be very loyal to the Old Guard was Warren G. Harding. When the party bosses needed an Ohio candidate to run for U.S. Senate in 1914, they chose Harding. He was distinguished and qualified. Party leaders knew that he could be trusted. Harding ran against Democratic candidate Timothy S. Hogan and Progressive candidate James R. Garfield.

Some people in the Republican Party ran a dirty campaign. They emphasized Hogan's Irish Catholic background, hoping to inflame voters' prejudice against his religion and ethnicity. (At the time, prejudice against Irish Americans and Catholics was common in the United States.) Although Harding did not personally stoop to such tactics, he benefited from them. He won the election by a large margin, getting 100,000 more votes than the Democratic candidate.

Among Harding's strongest supporters in the Republican Party was an attorney named Harry M. Daugherty. The two had first met at a Republican rally at the turn of the century. Although they had only chatted briefly, Daugherty was immediately taken with Harding's impressive voice and demeanor. As Harding

Harry M. Daugherty was the first politician to recognize Harding's full potential as a president.

✧ —————————

turned to walk away, Daugherty thought to himself, "What a great President he'd make!" From then on, Daugherty had predicted that he could help make Harding the nation's chief executive. Having Harding in the Senate was a first step.

As Daugherty came up with plans for Harding, more dramatic events were occurring elsewhere in the world. World War I (1914–1918) broke out in Europe. The conflict involved the Central powers—Germany, Austria-Hungary, and Turkey—and the Allies, led by Great Britain, France, and Russia. But President Wilson had promised to keep the United States out of the war. As Harding prepared for his six-year Senate term, which would begin in December 1915, foreign affairs did not weigh heavily on his mind.

He and Florence purchased a two-story brick home on Wyoming Avenue in Washington, D.C. Settling in the nation's capital proved to be easier for Warren

Harding than for his wife. Back home, Florence was known as one of Ohio's most successful businesswomen because of her management of the *Marion Star.* In Washington she was merely the wife of yet another new senator. After moving to Washington, Florence noted, "I wonder if anyone ever anticipated the coldness, the aloofness that one meets here at first [more than] in any other city of the world. It is indescribable. My home town was small and our neighbors were of the progressive and democratic citizenship type who cared little for form and more for achievement."

She tried to stay busy helping out in her husband's Senate office and doing small favors for his constituents (the people whom he was representing in Congress). They were often quite appreciative, and Florence felt at least somewhat useful. She had more time on her hands than most senators' wives,

✧ ——————————
Florence kept busy with sewing and other domestic tasks, as well as political causes such as women's right to vote.

who had children to raise. Since Florence had never become pregnant after marrying Warren, she assumed that he was unable to father a child.

Harding did not stand out as a senator. Many important pieces of legislation were debated and voted on while Harding was in Congress. But he had an extremely poor attendance record and missed more than two-thirds of the roll-call votes. Harding didn't even show up to vote on the woman suffrage amendment to the U.S. Constitution, which would give women in the United States the right to vote for the first time in history. Florence was firmly in

League of Women Voters

✧ ———————
Woman suffrage (women's right to vote) *was an important issue during Harding's term in the Senate.*

favor of woman suffrage, and Harding also claimed to be leaning toward supporting it.

He was present for the vote on the Prohibition amendment to the Constitution, though he was somewhat torn on the issue. Even though Harding enjoyed an occasional drink when out with friends, he felt the political pull from the Prohibition forces. He reluctantly voted in favor of the amendment. But rumor had it that he hoped enough states would hold off ratifying (approving) the amendment to defeat it.

That didn't happen. The Eighteenth Amendment to the Constitution was ratified in 1919, making Prohibition the law of the land. It was illegal to manufacture, sell, or transport alcohol in the United States. The Nineteenth Amendment to the Constitution, supporting woman suffrage, was also ratified and became law on August 18, 1920. U.S. women had won the right to vote without Warren G. Harding's help.

None of the 134 bills Harding introduced while in the Senate was considered especially noteworthy. Most dealt with local Ohio concerns. But, as he had in the past, Harding established good relationships with those he worked with. He often met with fellow senators behind the scenes to win their support for his proposed legislation. He was popular among the other senators. They saw him as someone they could count on to act reasonably in legislative disputes. Harding often reached out to Democrats as well as Republicans.

Secretary of State Josephus Daniels described Harding as "one of the most agreeable men with whom I ever came in contact, courteous and cordial." Harding was

Harding (second from right) enjoyed socializing with other senators.

———————————— ◇ ————————————

also considered fun. He frequently played golf or poker with other senators and always enjoyed a good joke. At the time, his mental outlook was good and the stress of being a senator did not seem to affect him.

THE FEMALE FACTOR

Harding also continued to be well liked by women he met. The tall, handsome senator, known for his charm and warm smile, was a favorite among women of all ages. But his youngest admirer was a teenage girl named Nan Britton. In 1910, when she was only fourteen, she had claimed to have fallen in love with Harding after seeing his campaign poster during his unsuccessful run for governor.

THE JAZZ AGE

The Jazz Age, also known as the Roaring Twenties, went down in history as a wild, "anything-goes" decade. Coming directly on the heels of World War I, the Jazz Age of the 1920s was a time to let loose and forget about the heartache of the recent war.

After Prohibition made making and selling liquor illegal, crime skyrocketed. Gangsters smuggled in alcohol from abroad, and people began going to illegal bars known as speakeasies. They listened and danced to a free-spirited new music called jazz, which was spreading like wildfire across the country.

Women, who had recently won the right to vote, became more assertive. Flappers, the name given to young women who traded in ladylike behavior for a more modern lifestyle, became a symbol of the Jazz Age. Flappers kept their hair short or bobbed, used makeup, and wore dresses that revealed not only their arms but also their legs from the knees down. These women, who were not bashful about asking gentlemen out, were known to dance the night away to lively ragtime tunes.

This flapper is dancing the Charleston, a dance that was popular in the 1920s.

The girl's father, Dr. Samuel Britton, practiced medicine in Marion and was friendly with Harding. To Britton's dismay, his daughter had plastered the walls of her room with Harding's campaign posters. She also wrote Harding's name all over her notebooks and tried to get a glimpse of him whenever she could. At times she even followed him home, making sure to stay far enough behind so as not to be seen.

It seemed as if the girl could think of little else. She continually talked about Harding to anyone who would listen. When word of Nan's feelings for Harding reached the Duchess, Florence appeared a bit annoyed, but not too upset at what she saw as a silly schoolgirl crush. Florence sarcastically told Nan's mother to tell her daughter that where Warren was concerned, "Distance lends enchantment."

Nan's parents tried to get her to lose interest in Harding. As far as they were concerned, the thought of them together was absurd. At the time, he was a forty-four-year-old married man, while Nan was a high school student. At one point, Nan's father visited Harding at the *Star* to see if the two of them could come up with a way to stop the teenager. But Nan remained obsessed with Harding. Though she had only met him once briefly, her infatuation continued through high school.

In 1917 Nan moved to New York City. She wrote to Harding asking if he remembered her and if he could help her find a job as a stenographer, or typist. Harding got her a job at a corporation in New York. The two met in New York, and they began an ongoing affair. She was twenty years old at the time, and he was fifty-one.

Harding's affair with
Nan Britton (right)
started after she moved
away from Marion.
———————————— ✧

Harding's affair with Nan Britton (right) started after she moved away from Marion.

Harding tried to be with Nan whenever he traveled for business or politics. Often the time they spent together was brief, but that didn't seem to lessen Nan's enthusiasm. Harding also wrote to her often. Some of his letters were as long as sixty pages. He told Nan that it had been many years since his "home situation had been satisfying."

In many ways, Harding found it easier to be with Nan than with Florence or Carrie. Nan was far more naive and less demanding. She liked that Warren was a politician and hoped that he would become president one day. Harding's relationship with Nan seriously jeopardized that possibility, however. If the public learned of his extramarital affair with the young woman, the scandal would doubtless destroy a bid for office. Nevertheless, he was willing to take the risk.

He had some close calls, though. Once Nan and Harding met at a New York hotel, where Harding had registered under the name Mr. Hardwick. Nan recalled later that she was wearing a short pink dress that made her look even younger than she was. It is against the law for an adult man to have a sexual relationship with a girl under age eighteen. Apparently the hotel detectives suspected that Nan was underage. The detectives burst into the couple's hotel room and found them in bed. The detectives insisted on knowing Nan's name and age. She described what happened next: "I remember he [Harding] told them I was twenty-one years old, and I, not realizing that he wanted to make me as old as he safely could, interrupted him and stated truthfully that I was only twenty."

✧ ——————————
This is what New York City looked like when Nan was living there in the early 1900s.

At that point, one of the detectives saw Harding's real name inside his hat. Realizing that he was a senator, the detectives suddenly became apologetic. They were eager to keep the senator out of trouble. They even helped the pair sneak out of the hotel the back way. Harding gave the men twenty dollars for their trouble. As he and Nan left in a taxi, Harding remarked, "I thought I wouldn't get out of that [for] under $1000!"

SURPRISING NEWS

Harding continued to see Nan at least one night a week, scheduling visits when he had to travel for government business. Toward the end of February 1919, Nan wrote to him to say that she was pregnant. Harding was taken by surprise. Since he and the Duchess had not had children together, he didn't think he could have children.

Though Harding was shaken, he tried to remain calm. He met with Nan and told her, "We must go at this thing in a sane way, dearie, and we must not allow ourselves to be nervous over it." Yet Harding was actually quite nervous. He suggested that Nan take some of the Dr. Humphrey #11 pills he'd brought with him. Suspecting that the pills might abort the baby, Nan refused. She wanted the child and was determined to give birth. Harding realized that this could ruin his political future. He was also aware that the Duchess would "raise hell" if she knew.

But Harding went along with what Nan wanted. He told her that she was "the perfect sweetheart and the perfect mother." Unlike Harding, Nan was thrilled about being pregnant. She referred to the unborn baby as "the young lieutenant."

Nan's sister, who was far more practical, urged Nan to have an abortion. Harding hinted at the same thing in his next few letters to her. But nothing could make Nan change her mind. She became increasingly protective of the baby she was carrying. Not quite sure how to proceed, Harding began to support Nan financially. First, he found a small apartment for her in New York. Once her pregnancy began to show, Nan moved to the New Jersey seaside resort of Asbury Park. No one knew

———————————— ◇ ————————————

Nan went to Asbury Park, New Jersey, (below) so that no one would know about her pregnancy.

her there, and she used a false name. While she was in New Jersey, Harding avoided seeing Nan. But he made sure that she had as much money as she needed.

On October 22, 1919, Nan gave birth to a baby girl she named Elizabeth Ann. Harding avoided seeing her, both for personal and political reasons.

*Harding didn't expect to run for president in 1920, but
unforeseen events pushed him into the race.*

CHAPTER FIVE

THE BIG STEP FORWARD

The only thing I really worry about is that I might be nominated and elected. That's an awful thing to contemplate.

—Warren G. Harding, referring to the presidency

In 1919 it didn't look as though Warren G. Harding would be the Republican Party's candidate for president in the upcoming 1920 election. Former president Theodore Roosevelt still hoped to recapture the presidency. Although Roosevelt had left the Republican Party in 1912 and started the Progressive Party, he had since come back into the fold as a party member. He seemed to be the Republicans' best hope for a presidential win in 1920.

The Republicans were feeling confident about their chances of winning back the White House from the Democrats. In 1916 Democrat Woodrow Wilson had narrowly won a second term as president with a promise to

The United States was drawn into World War I when three
of its ships were attacked by German submarines like the one above.

———————————— ✧ ————————————

keep the United States out of World War I. Then, on
March 18, 1917, German submarines torpedoed three
U.S. merchant ships, the *City of Memphis,* the *Illinois,*
and the *Vigilancia.* Many U.S. citizens were killed.

Wilson felt that the United States could no longer
remain neutral. On April 2, 1917, he asked Congress to
declare war on Germany. The president's request sparked
patriotic enthusiasm in the United States. As the issue of
war was debated in Congress, seventeen senators spoke in
favor of going to war. Harding was among them. The
United States declared war on Germany on April 6.

Germany and its allies surrendered in November
1918. Wilson went to Paris the following spring to help
work out an enduring peace. He came back to the
United States and asked the Senate to ratify an interna-

tional peace treaty known as the Treaty of Versailles. The treaty contained plans for a League of Nations, an organization to promote peace and security among nations of the world.

Wilson, who was instrumental in designing the league, won the Nobel Peace Prize for his work in 1919. But the Republicans, who held the majority in Congress, took a more isolationist (hands off) approach to foreign relations. Preferring to keep the United States out of international affairs, Republican senators, including Harding, opposed U.S. involvement in Wilson's proposed League of Nations. The Senate voted down the Treaty of Versailles by seven votes.

───────────────── ✧ ─────────────────

The League of Nations was set up after World War I to maintain world peace. The first session (below) took place in November 1920.

Wilson was dismayed. He saw U.S. support for the League of Nations as crucial to the world's future. To drum up support for the treaty, he went on a nationwide speaking tour. Against his doctor's orders, Wilson traveled eight thousand miles in twenty-two days, giving thirty-eight speeches. Exhausted, he suffered a stroke, which left him partially paralyzed. As a result, he was unable to run for president in 1920. The stage was set for the Republicans to take the presidency.

Harding knew that Theodore Roosevelt would be a leading Republican candidate for the presidency, so he tried to link himself politically to Roosevelt. After Harding had written Roosevelt several complimentary letters, the former president agreed to meet with him to discuss ways to bolster the Republican Party. Following their get-together, Harding wrote, "We did not dwell on the differences of 1912, for that was an old story."

MAJOR CHANGES

The political scene shifted dramatically on January 6, 1919. That morning Theodore Roosevelt died in his sleep of a heart blockage. Many political figures, including Harding, attended the funeral. Yet while some wept and mourned the loss of a great Republican, others were already looking ahead to the future.

Expert political schemer Harry Daugherty had long felt that Harding had an appealing presence and could win the presidency. And Daugherty saw himself as the man who could shape Harding's presidential potential. Daugherty said of Harding, "I found him, sunning himself, like a turtle on a log, and I pushed him into the water."

Daugherty had no illusions about his candidate. He knew that Harding was not likely to be the first choice of most party members. He also knew that Harding lacked the political backing to win the presidential nomination. Daugherty did not want to alienate the Republican Old Guard. Therefore, in raising support for his choice, Daugherty never asked key party members to vote for Harding in the nomination process. Instead, he suggested that they vote for Harding as a second choice if their first choice was unable to win the nomination.

When a Harding supporter suggested that more needed to be done, an associate of Daugherty reassuringly told him, "You haven't heard that Harding is making any enemies anywhere, have you? That's the answer. Harding will be nominated."

Daugherty explained his strategy for getting Harding on the ticket to a group of newspaper reporters several months before the Republican National Convention: "I don't expect Senator Harding to be nominated on the first, second, or third ballot, but I think about eleven minutes after two o'clock on Friday morning of the convention, when fifteen or twenty men, bleary-eyed and perspiring profusely from the heat, are sitting around a table, some one of them will say: 'Who will we nominate?' At the decisive time the friends of Senator Harding can suggest him and can afford to abide by the result. I don't know but what I might suggest him myself."

Daugherty hoped to make Harding the perfect compromise candidate. When the convention reached a deadlock, as Daugherty was sure it would, Harding would have his chance to shine.

CONTENDERS FOR THE NOMINATION

The two main contenders for the 1920 Republican presidential nomination were the front-runner, General Leonard Wood, and Governor Frank O. Lowden of Illinois. Wood was a doctor from New England who had joined the U.S. Army Medical Corps in 1885. In his twenty-four years in the army, he had risen through the ranks to become a general. A former Progressive, Wood had been very close to Theodore Roosevelt. Even though Roosevelt and his Progressive followers had rejoined the Republicans, many Old Guard party members still hesitated to support the former Progressives.

Behind the scenes, Wood's manager had begun trying to win over the party bosses. He approached Boies Penrose from Pennsylvania, who was considered a boss among bosses; Will Hays, chairman of the National Republican Committee; and George Harvey, editor of the *North American Review,* who held a great deal of sway within the party. When Wood realized what was going on, he fired his manager, insisting that he wanted no part of any shady business. Believing that Wood might be too honest to work with, many party bosses began to have doubts about backing him for the presidency.

Illinois governor Frank O. Lowden, the other leading candidate for the nomination, had also been a Progressive. He had a reputation as still being something of a reformer. A number of party members feared that he too might be difficult to work with.

By the time the convention opened in Chicago on June 8, 1920, neither leading candidate appeared to have a clear majority. This became obvious once the delegates started

General Leonard Wood (left) *was an honest politician.*

voting, a process that took several days. After four ballots, there still wasn't a winner. Wood seemed to be picking up votes as the ballots progressed. At that point, he was only 177 votes short of the 491 needed to capture the nomination. Harding was much farther down the line.

Wood's lead greatly upset some of the Old Guard, who feared that Wood might not cooperate with them once he was in office. To stop his momentum, the bosses declared that a deadlock had been reached. The balloting was stopped, and the convention was adjourned until the following morning, Saturday, June 12.

At the beginning of the 1920 Republican Convention (above), it was unclear who would become the Republican candidate for the presidential campaign.

———————— ✧ ————————

THE SMOKE-FILLED ROOM

Meanwhile, that night dozens of key party members got together behind closed doors in what Daugherty referred to as "a smoke-filled room." Their goal was to choose a winner. Many names were brought up and eventually eliminated. A number of potential nominees were dismissed because of their Progressive backgrounds. The platform (declaration of principles and policies) created for the Republican candidate to run on was very conservative. It favored big business by supporting both lower taxes for U.S. businesses and high tariffs on imported goods. The platform also proposed restrictions on immigration and organized labor. The bosses in the meeting wanted to be sure they had a candidate who represented these views.

In the end, only one candidate was left who had done nothing to lose favor with the Old Guard. It was the candidate who seemed to be everyone's second choice—Warren G. Harding. George Harvey later described Harding as the most logical choice, since he would readily go along with the Republican majority in Congress. Senator Frank Brandegee from Connecticut told a small group of newspaper reporters how the delegates arrived at Harding: "There ain't any first-raters this year. This ain't 1880 or 1904; we haven't any John Shermans or Theodore Roosevelts; we got a lot of second-raters and Warren Harding is the best of the second-raters."

DOUBTS

It is difficult to know how much Harding himself wanted the nomination. For months before the national convention, he had discouraged his friends and acquaintances from promoting his candidacy. Once he even wrote to a friend that he would be "unhappy every hour" if he entered the presidential race.

An incident the night before the final vote also gave him pause. The powerful party members who were deciding on the nomination called Harding into the room. They said, "We think you may be nominated tomorrow; before acting finally, we think you should tell us, on your conscience and before God, whether there is anything that might be brought up against you that would embarrass the party, any impediment [obstacle] that might disqualify you or make you inexpedient [unwise], either as candidate or as President."

At first, Harding seemed taken aback. He asked for a few minutes to reflect on it and left the room. He returned just ten minutes later. With a smile on his face, he assured his supporters that there was nothing. As a man with a young mistress and an illegitimate daughter, Harding was taking a tremendous risk with his answer. Although he had never met his child, he still saw Nan occasionally. He figured he could get away with it, since Nan and their daughter were a well-guarded secret. Florence had heard rumors about Nan, but at that point, even she didn't know for sure.

Although Florence Harding had a reputation for pushing her husband, she did not strongly urge him to pursue the presidency. In the months before the convention, she had been doubtful that her husband could win the nomination. The day before the balloting began, Florence told a friend, "I don't know why we're keeping the [campaign] headquarters. It's simply a needless expense." That same day, she was quoted in a newspaper, saying, "I cannot see why anyone should want to be President . . . . I can see but one word written over the head of my husband, if he is elected and that word is 'Tragedy.'"

THE REPUBLICANS' CHOICE

Party bosses made it possible for Harding to become the top candidate for the nomination. Yet he did have some qualities that made him a desirable choice among other Republicans. They knew that Harding was loyal, reasonable, and able to get along well with others. These qualities, along with his elegant bearing and winning smile, made Harding an appropriate candidate for some. Harding was also quite intelligent. However, because he was so anxious to be liked and accepted, he often let others think for him.

The convention delegates nominated Harding on June 12 on the tenth ballot. Governor Calvin Coolidge of Massachusetts was nominated as his running mate.

Harding (left) with his running mate, Calvin Coolidge

✧ ——————————

Whatever Warren and Florence Harding's doubts were at first, the couple rose to the occasion once the nomination was made. They enjoyed the support of most of the Republican Party. The Republican press ran enthusiastic headlines and descriptions of Harding. An article in the *Atlanta Constitution* summed up the positive feeling: "As for Senator Harding, he will unquestioningly make a strong candidate. His chief strength lies in the fact that he has been a sort of a middle-of-the-roader. . . . The Republicans might have gone further and done much worse."

The future looked bright for Harding and the Duchess. But there was one last problem to resolve before the campaign began. Some influential Republicans had learned of Harding's former relationship with Carrie Phillips. Although Harding and Carrie had not seen each other for years, the party leaders did not want the Democrats to find out about the affair.

A representative of the party went to visit Carrie and Jim Phillips. They were offered twenty thousand dollars in cash, plus a monthly allowance for as long as Harding was in office if he won the election, in return for their cooperation in keeping quiet. The money came from a fund donated by Republican Party members. Harding was aware of the offer and did not object. Carrie and her husband were also given an all-expenses-paid luxury cruise around the world. The only condition was that they had to leave immediately and could not return before the election.

Carrie and Jim Phillips accepted the offer. While they prepared for the trip of a lifetime, Warren G. Harding prepared for the campaign that would set him on the journey of his lifetime.

CHAPTER SIX

THE CAMPAIGN

*America's present need is not
heroics, but healing.*
—Warren G. Harding, 1920

Harding began his campaign for the presidency at a difficult time in the United States. World War I had ended. Returning soldiers had come home to an economic slump, with rising prices of goods and high unemployment. Numerous businesses had failed, and many people, unable to pay their mortgages (loans), lost their homes. Tensions ran high in cities such as Washington, D.C., where race riots had broken out. The Ku Klux Klan and other racist groups unfairly blamed African Americans for nearly everything that was wrong in the nation.

Harding focused his campaign on improving life in the United States. His slogan promised a "return to normalcy," which was meant to suggest the peacefulness and stability that many people believed the country had enjoyed before

*Unemployeed New Yorkers (above) contributed to the feeling of unrest
that was in the United States when Harding became president.*

————————————— ✧ —————————————

the war. Whether or not the good old days were really so
good, Americans longed to believe in the ideal that
Republicans were selling in 1920.

President Woodrow Wilson was too weak to run for
another term in office following his stroke. So the Democrats
chose James M. Cox, governor of Ohio, as their presidential
candidate. Cox shared many of Wilson's views, including his
hope for U.S. participation in the League of Nations.

Many of Harding's campaign speeches stressed that
President Wilson had been too involved in international
affairs. Harding argued that trying to establish world peace

would only use up U.S. resources. Harding promised that, if elected, he would concentrate on domestic matters. He told voters about his "American First" plan:

"It is fine to idealize, but it is very practical to make sure our own house is in perfect order before we attempt the miracle of the Old-World stabilization.

"Call it the selfishness of nationality if you will, I think it an inspiration to the patriotic devotion—

"To safeguard America first.

"To stabilize America first.

"To prosper America first.

"To think of America first.

"To exalt [glorify] America first.

"To live for and revere [honor] America first."

✦ ———————

This political cartoon from the 1920 presidential campaign criticized Harding's "America First" plan.

*Harding became known for his presidential campaigning
from the front porch of his home in Marion, Ohio.*

THE FRONT PORCH CAMPAIGN

From the end of July 1920 through the end of September,
Harding ran what was known as the "front porch campaign." Basically, he did much of his stumping from his
own front porch at his home in Marion, Ohio. (Warren
and Florence had kept their house in Marion while living
in Washington, D.C.) Brass bands played as an assortment
of groups and reporters appeared on the Hardings' front
lawn every day to hear the Republican candidate speak.
Harding also arranged to meet individually with many
special-interest delegations, including African Americans,
farmers, businesspeople, veterans, and others.

During Harding's front porch campaign, more than 600,000 people came to see him in Marion. The Republican Party also invited many sympathetic newspaper reporters to town to report on the wonderful potential of this candidate who was in direct touch with the people.

Harding's speeches tended to dwell less on specific policies than on simple promises to lower the cost of living and decrease unemployment. Harding also stressed the need for people to help one another, noting, "Out of such relations grow mutual respect, mutual sympathy, and mutual interests, without which life holds little of real enjoyment."

While conducting his front porch campaign, Harding projected the image of a dignified, all-American family man who loved his home and his country. For two and a half months, he kissed babies, shook hands with countless visitors, and smiled broadly.

───────────────── ✦
Harding met many people while he was on the campaign trail.

Harding portrayed his life in Marion as wholesome and happy. It was a lifestyle that many people longed for, and it made them feel good about Harding.

Harding's Republican Party advisers carefully planned his every move. The candidate was instructed to be polite, never to become flustered, and to avoid taking firm stands on controversial issues. All his front porch speeches were written for him ahead of time, to avoid Harding's tendency to go on and on, or "bloviate." Harding commented, "I could make better speeches than these, but I have to be so careful."

The front porch campaign was highly successful. But by mid-September, Harding's campaign advisers decided that he needed more national exposure. So, toward the campaign's end, Harding left his home base of Marion to conduct a speaking tour. The trip took him through Minnesota, Illinois, West Virginia, Pennsylvania, Maryland, Nebraska, Kansas, Oklahoma, Iowa, Missouri, Tennessee, Kentucky, and New York.

ON THE CAMPAIGN TRAIL

As Harding campaigned around the country, citizens learned more about what the Ohio senator stood for. Harding told audiences that he believed in careful spending in government, and he vowed to limit federal spending. Harding was extremely pro-farmer and wanted to create an emergency tariff to protect farm products from foreign competition. He also proposed restricting immigration, expanding the navy, and creating a merchant marine (a national fleet of commercial ships). Addressing the ongoing racial violence in the United States, Harding talked about passing a law against lynching (illegal executions, usually by mobs). He hoped for other laws as well to protect the rights of African Americans. He also wanted to see more African Americans appointed to federal offices.

By October 1920, Harding's national popularity had surged. The vice-presidential candidate, Calvin Coolidge, had also done some traveling to win votes. Coolidge had campaigned throughout New England and the South.

Meanwhile, Harding's Democratic opponent, James M. Cox, had not waged a very successful campaign. Cox was not as well known as Harding. While Harding was seen as a family man, Cox was divorced. Even though Florence Harding had been married once before, her divorce did not become an issue in the campaign. Cox was also a strong supporter of the League of Nations at a time when many people in the United States were more interested in improving conditions at home than in international relations. All these factors worked against Cox and in Harding's favor.

Harding's campaign was not completely free of problems, however. The old questions about his racial background came up. This time the rumors

——————————— ✧

James M. Cox was the Democratic candidate for the 1920 presidential election.

Warren and Florence (third and fourth from left)
line up to vote on November 2, 1920.

———————————— ◇ ————————————

were spread by William Estabrook Chancellor, a professor of economics, politics, and social sciences at the College of Wooster in Ohio. Chancellor was a white supremacist who believed that the white race was superior to all others.

Chancellor had leaflets printed up charging that Harding was "not a white man." Chancellor distributed the leaflets just a few weeks before election day. Harding was furious at what he considered a low blow that would heighten racial tensions. Most newspapers refused to print the charges, however, and the Democratic Party ignored them.

November 2, 1920, was both Warren G. Harding's fifty-fifth birthday and election day. That morning he and the

Duchess voted after breakfast. It was the first election in which women had the right to vote. Florence was the first woman to vote for her husband for president. Harding waited in line for fifteen minutes to vote. Others offered to let him go to the head of the line, but he refused.

When the couple returned home, Harding was pleased to find that his wife had arranged a surprise birthday party for him. There were gifts and a white cake with fifty-five pink candles. But the best present of all came from the American people. They elected him president of the United States. Harding won thirty-seven states, while Cox carried only eleven. As one political observer noted, "It wasn't a landslide, it was an earthquake."

Florence Harding always played an active role in her husband's political career, and this continued when she became First Lady.

CHAPTER SEVEN

CHIEF EXECUTIVE

I have no trouble with my enemies, I can take care of my enemies all right. It's my friends that keep me up at night.
—Warren G. Harding

The Hardings were somewhat nervous about moving into the White House. Florence had observed a couple of years earlier, "I've seen the inside of the White House [the work and pressure of the presidency]. The office is killing Wilson as surely as if he had been stabbed at his desk." The Duchess was determined that the presidency would not take such a heavy toll on her husband. She made it clear that she would be an active participant in how things were run. As one reporter noted, "Anyone who tries to figure the Harding of the next four years without counting the influence of Mrs. Harding will get a wrong result. They have been, are and will continue to be full partners."

In many ways, Florence Harding was an inspiring First Lady and a real help to her husband. She brought vigor and new ideas to the job of First Lady. Florence firmly believed that the White House belonged to the people, and she opened it up to the public at every opportunity. She arranged social or official events at the White House most nights. The Duchess also encouraged more tourists to visit. To the guests' amazement, the First Lady frequently came out to meet and shake hands with them.

But Florence did more than just meet and greet White House visitors. She also worked actively for women's rights, animal rights, and veterans' rights. Mrs. Harding regularly visited veterans' hospitals to cheer up the men and listen to their concerns.

President Harding also embraced his new job with gusto, although the rigors of the presidency often proved difficult for him. With a great deal to learn and many important decisions to make, Harding sometimes felt overwhelmed by his responsibilities. As he once told William Allen White, the editor of the Emporia (Kansas) *Gazette,* "I can't make a . . . thing out of this tax problem. I listen to one side and they seem right, and then . . . I talk to the other side and they seem just as right, and here I am where I started. I know somewhere there is a book that will give me the truth, but . . . I couldn't read the book."

As president, Harding saw much less of Nan Britton. She could not come to the White House very often, because that would look suspicious. Harding was also extremely busy and very much in the public's eye. When Nan did visit, the only private place Harding could find for them to be together was a large coat closet. Harding continued to financially support Nan and Elizabeth Ann. But he still refused to meet his daughter.

ACHIEVEMENTS IN OFFICE

Harding played golf twice a week and enjoyed poker games at the White House with old friends. Some critics called him a lazy president who failed to put in the effort the position required. However, this was far from the truth. Harding worked long days that began at eight in the morning and often did not end until after midnight. Each day was filled with meetings, appointments, official events and ceremonies, and social engagements.

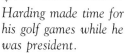

Harding made time for his golf games while he was president.

People lined up each day for a chance to speak with President Harding.
———————— ✧ ————————

Nearly every day at noon, Harding made time to meet with the public. He shook hands, smiled, and listened carefully to what people had to say. Harding had always had an easy way with people, and these sessions seemed to renew his spirit. He often stayed up until the early hours of the morning answering letters from ordinary citizens. Having run a newspaper, Harding was open to talking to reporters and held press conferences twice a week.

Some of Harding's achievements in office were more obvious. He created the Bureau of the Budget and significantly reduced the federal debt. He also eased taxes on individuals as well as businesses, and he started the Veterans' Bureau (later renamed the Veterans Administration). The Veterans' Bureau was intended to provide war veterans and their families with benefits and services, such as health care, pensions, education, home loans, life insurance, and job training.

Harding Fast Facts

Warren G. Harding was the first president to:
- listen to the presidential election returns over the radio;
- ride to his inauguration in a car;
- have his inaugural address broadcast over an amplification system;
- give a speech in the South promoting civil rights;
- have a speech broadcast over the radio *(right)*;
- be elected on his birthday.

Florence Harding was:
- the first First Lady to ride in an airplane;
- the first First Lady to vote;
- considered the model for the modern First Lady.

Other Harding facts:
- The Hardings had an Airedale terrier dog named Laddie Boy and a pet finch named Pete.
- Warren G. Harding's favorite meal was waffles covered with chipped beef and gravy.
- Harding's middle name, Gamaliel, means "God is my reward" in Hebrew.
- Florence Harding excelled at horseback riding.

The twenty-ninth president made some important strides in foreign affairs as well. Harding organized an international arms limitation meeting, called the Washington Conference, from November 1921 to February 1922. The nations represented at the conference—the United States, Great Britain, France, Italy, and Japan—signed treaties limiting and reducing their naval strength. The conference delegates agreed to limit the number and size of their new warships as well as reduce the fleets they already had by voluntarily sinking some of the ships. As the first international disarmament meeting of its kind, the conference received worldwide acclaim.

Overall, Harding tended to take a narrower view of the presidency than many of the presidents who came before him. Harding had a deep respect for the right of Congress to function independently without pressure from the executive branch. He was a firm believer in the separation of power among different branches of government. In Harding's opinion, presidents who tried to force their views on Congress did the country a disservice.

Instead, Harding saw the role of president as largely ceremonial. While some presidents shunned the pomp and ceremony that comes with the office, Harding reveled in it. He believed in leaving the political debates and arguments to Congress. Harding felt that the president of the United States must first and foremost be respected. This would be impossible if "the chief executive entered the political arena like an armed gladiator." He added, "Only a president who was loved could properly retain the public faith and be a symbol of national pride and confidence."

Harding (front left) *enjoyed the ceremonial aspects of the presidency, such as this appearance at a state fair.*

────────────────── ✧ ──────────────────

If the president did get involved in political disputes, Harding said, it should be in the role of arbitrator. Through the years, he had prided himself on being able to bring different groups together. He hoped to be assisted in this task by loyal advisers on whom he could rely for objective, honest information.

Many of the people he chose for these roles came from Ohio and had known Harding for years. The group became known as "the Ohio Gang." It included Harry M. Daugherty, Harding's presidential campaign manager, who became attorney general (the chief legal adviser of the United States) after Harding took office. Frank Edgar (Ed) Scobey, the former sheriff of Miami County, Ohio, became director of the U.S.

Harding (left) sits with his advisers. Daugherty (third from left) was attorney general. Vice President Coolidge is at the far end of the table.

————————————— ✧ —————————————

Mint (where money is manufactured). Dick Crissinger, Harding's boyhood friend from Marion, was named governor of the Federal Reserve System (the U.S. central bank).

Harding had always been honest as a public official, and he assumed that anyone he appointed to assist him would uphold the same values. As Harding's physician, Dr. Charles Sawyer, noted, "Mr. Harding had a friendly feeling for all mankind, but those to whom he gave his confidence and those with whom he really associated intimately were always selected with the belief that they were honorable and upright."

SCANDALS AND CORRUPTION

Some of Harding's advisers lacked his political integrity. They betrayed his trust by involving the Harding administration in scandals that affected how his presidency would be viewed throughout history. One of the most shocking incidents was known as the Teapot Dome scandal. Albert B. Fall, Harding's secretary of the interior (the person in charge of preserving the nation's natural resources), had become deeply in debt after purchasing more land than he could afford. Needing money, Fall accepted bribes of more than $400,000 in cash and bonds to lease government-owned oil reserves to private companies. (The major oil field involved was the Teapot Dome Reserve in Wyoming.) Once the truth was exposed through Senate committee hearings, the public was outraged. Fall was eventually tried, convicted, and sentenced to prison.

Another scandal in Harding's administration centered on Charles R. Forbes, the director of the Veterans' Bureau. Warren and Florence Harding had first met Forbes in 1915 on a visit to Hawaii. Forbes was there overseeing the construction of the naval base at Pearl Harbor. When he was put in charge of the newly created, well-funded Veterans' Bureau, Forbes could have made an important difference in the health and welfare of the nation's former soldiers. But he was more interested in helping himself. Forbes sold government medical

——————————— ✧
Charles R. Forbes

supplies to his friends at ridiculously low prices. He falsely claimed that these products had been purchased for World War I and had deteriorated in storage.

This was not Forbes's only shady deal. In 1922 Congress approved spending $17 million to build twelve new veterans' hospitals. In return for bribes, Forbes authorized the purchase of land for the facilities at a highly inflated cost. He also accepted cash to give some construction companies a better chance to win building contracts when they were awarded.

Harding was shocked when he learned of Forbes's illegal activities. The president reportedly called Forbes to the White House and shook him like a rag doll. Hoping to avoid a public scandal, Harding allowed Forbes to travel to Europe. While Forbes was out of the country, the president asked for his resignation. But the trouble wasn't over. A later Senate investigation was followed by a trial. Forbes was convicted and sent to prison.

Forbes had involved Charles Cramer, the general counsel (lawyer) for the Veterans' Bureau, in his dishonest dealings. Once the scandal surfaced, Cramer could not handle the stress. He shot himself in the head.

In May 1923, two months after Cramer's suicide, another Harding associate, Jesse W. Smith, also took his own life. Smith was an old friend of Attorney General Daugherty. Smith had been arranging illegal settlements allowed criminals to get away with breaking the law. Daugherty was later accused of cheating the government out of money, but after two juries were unable to reach a verdict, he was freed.

Through bribes, political favors, and help from old friends, the wrongdoers in Harding's administration kept the brewing scandals from reaching the press and the public. Harding, however, often learned of these disasters, and the knowledge tore him apart. He wasn't sure what action he should take and what would be best for his administration and the country.

In a private meeting with Secretary of Commerce Herbert Hoover, Harding asked him what he would do if he were president and had been told of a scandal that was about to surface. Hoover responded, "Publish it, and at least get credit for integrity on your side."

When Hoover pressed him for more details, Harding admitted that he'd discovered some serious irregularities in the Justice Department that centered on Jesse Smith. The president confided that he had sent for Smith to tell him that he'd be arrested the next morning. Harding later learned that Smith did not wait for that to happen. That night he burned all his papers and committed suicide.

When Hoover asked if Harry Daugherty was involved, Harding avoided the question and changed the subject. The discussion was over, but Harding remained tormented about how he should handle such problems.

Although Harding was not guilty of any official misconduct, the actions of those in his administration reflected poorly on him. But even before the scandals became publicly known, Harding realized that he had to do something to turn things around. Tired of his old political buddies' antics, the president seemed ready for more independent action. As he looked ahead to the upcoming presidential election in 1924, Harding decided to reach out to the people. As Samuel Hopkins Adams, a reporter who often wrote about White House events, remarked, "Something new was stirring in him."

*Harding (left) and Florence start out on their
cross-country trip west.*

CHAPTER EIGHT

THE VOYAGE
OF UNDERSTANDING

We have been having a wonderful trip
across the Continent. . . . I am very much
more proud of our country than I
was when I started westward.
—Warren G. Harding

In the spring of 1923, Harding decided to take an extended cross-country trip that he called the Voyage of Understanding. He would travel by train through the Midwest, the West, and then take a ship north to Alaska, talking to citizens throughout the country about their concerns. Accompanying Harding was a large group that included his wife, his doctor, reporters and photographers, and several White House aides.

At first, things seemed to go quite well. Harding received favorable publicity as he ventured westward. Stopping in numerous small towns, he gave speeches from his train platform to enthusiastic crowds that gathered to see him.

Harding spoke in favor of a World Court that would help nations cooperate and work together on international concerns. His support for the World Court appealed to people who had been in favor of the League of Nations. It was also a dramatic break from the views of the Republican Old Guard. But Harding was ready to follow his own new vision. In a speech he wrote himself, Harding told audiences, "My soul yearns for peace. My heart is anguished by the sufferings of war. My spirit is eager to serve. My passion is for justice over force. My hope is in the great court. My mind is made up. My resolution is fixed."

Harding addressed thousands of people on the trip. He usually spoke outdoors, and he refused to let a blistering heat wave slow him down. But as the journey continued, Harding's doctor, Charles Sawyer, grew concerned. A couple of years earlier, the president had begun to show signs of heart disease, and this trip seemed to exhaust him. When the president's train pulled into Kansas City, Missouri, a reporter noted that Harding's "lips were swollen and blue, his eyes puffed, and his hands seemed stiff." Sawyer cautioned the president to slow down, but Harding ignored his advice.

FAILING HEALTH

As the trip continued, Harding grew weaker. It was harder for him to move around, and at times his speech seemed strained. Sawyer again warned Harding to slow the tour's pace. The doctor was concerned about Harding's heart. Harding was tiring easily and occasionally experienced chest pains. Nevertheless, Harding still ignored the warnings.

Harding (left), *the governor of Alaska* (center), *and Florence* (right) *dress warmly for the Alaska climate.*

———————————————— ✧ ————————————————

After traveling through Washington State, Harding's group boarded a ship for the trip to Alaska. Harding said that he hoped his plan for a World Court would catch on and that his administration would be remembered as a "period of understanding."

But his plans and hopes soon unraveled. During the voyage along the Alaska coast, a seaplane (an airplane that can take off and land on water) met the ship to deliver an important message to Harding. A reporter remembered, "After reading it, [Harding] suffered something like a collapse." Although the contents of the message were never revealed, some historians believe that Harding had received word of another breaking scandal.

Those traveling with the president noted that his health and morale worsened significantly. After the ship returned to the mainland, Harding had trouble continuing his speaking tour. When he addressed a group in Seattle, Washington, he seemed dazed and began to slur his words. At one point, he referred to Alaska as Nebraska. That night Harding suffered from extreme indigestion. Some people thought it might have been the crabmeat he had eaten, but Harding's doctor feared that the president had had a heart attack. Yet because Sawyer was not a heart specialist, a precise diagnosis was never made.

LAST STOP

Although the journey continued, Harding agreed to stop making speeches for a while. When the group arrived in San Francisco, California, on Sunday, July 29, the president claimed to feel better. But those with him felt that he looked seriously ill. A heart specialist was called in, and Harding was confined to his bed in the Palace Hotel.

On Monday, Harding was running a temperature of 102 degrees. Another specialist was brought in, and Harding was diagnosed with bronchial pneumonia. As the days passed, Harding seemed to improve. By Wednesday he was eating solid food again and reading the newspapers. On Thursday he began making plans to return to the White House later in the week. He also received some visitors that day. He told one that he regretted not catching any fish in Alaska. That evening the Duchess read her husband a flattering article about him in the *Saturday Evening Post.* Harding said, "That's good. Go on, read some more." Those were his last words. Warren G. Harding died that night, August 2, 1923.

EPILOGUE

When news of Harding's death reached the public, there was a tremendous outpouring of grief across the nation. He had been a popular president, and news of the scandals surrounding his administration hadn't yet become public. Harding's body was transported by train from California back to Washington, D.C. As the train passed, people stood by the tracks to pay their last respects to the president. Whenever the train stopped, mourners rushed up to bring funeral bouquets. The train pulled into Washington filled with flowers.

Historians, however, have generally not praised Warren G. Harding's presidency. Harding has come in last in nearly every poll on presidential achievement. Yet some authors argue that Harding was just coming into his own when he died. Had he lived to finish his term in office, he might have achieved more.

It is difficult to know what might have happened or how Harding might have been remembered differently. Shortly after his death, many of the scandals involving his administration came to light. Harding's reputation also suffered because of his extramarital relationships. Nan Britton wrote a book entitled *The President's Daughter,* in which she exposed the fact that Harding had a child outside his marriage. Love letters that Harding wrote to Carrie Phillips were eventually uncovered as well. In time, few people seemed to remember Harding with a great deal of respect or fondness.

NAN BRITTON

Although Harding financially supported Nan Britton and his child *(right)* while he was alive, he left no money for them in his will. This put Britton in a difficult position. Looking for a new man to help support her, she married a ship captain in January 1924. But Nan's husband failed to give her either the money or the emotional comfort she sought. As a result, Nan had the marriage annulled (declared invalid).

After that, Nan visited one of Harding's sisters to ask for financial assistance. Nan hoped for a sizable amount of money from Harding's family, but they refused to give her anything. At that point, she wrote a tell-all book, *The President's Daughter.* The book caused a scandal—and brought Nan the cash she was hoping for. At least temporarily, she did not have to worry about money.

Once her book earnings were spent, Nan and her daughter settled into a somewhat ordinary life. Nan found a job at an employment agency in Evanston, Illinois, where Elizabeth Ann graduated from high school and then married. She moved to California with her husband, and the couple had three children.

Harding's funeral train crossed the country from California back to Washington, D.C.

One person who did deeply miss the president was Florence Harding, who took the loss of her husband particularly hard. While she tried to keep up a brave front, her close friends knew how upset she was. Florence often visited her husband's tomb and developed a special fondness for the twenty-six enlisted men who were assigned to guard it.

Soon after Harding's death, Florence faced her own decline in health. She died on Novermber 21, 1924, after suffering from serious heart and kidney problems for months.

The Harding Memorial

Following Harding's death, the Harding Memorial Association was established by several of the former president's friends. Organizers hoped to raise funds to build a Harding Memorial (*below*) in Marion, Ohio. At first, donations for the memorial poured in. Schoolchildren from across the nation sent in their nickels and dimes. Community groups held potluck dinners to raise money for the structure. However, as scandals connected to Harding's administration continued to surface, donations dropped off somewhat.

The association was able to construct the memorial a few years after Harding's death. Made of Georgian marble, the monument is a classic Greek open-air structure. Set in a spacious park area in Marion, Ohio, it is more than fifty feet tall and has forty-six columns. In December 1927, the bodies of President and Mrs. Harding were buried in the monument.

Just before slipping into unconsciousness on the day she died, Florence asked for her checkbook. Her last act was to write a check for $125 to pay for a Thanksgiving dinner with all the trimmings for the men guarding her husband's tomb.

Some of Warren G. Harding's problems may have resulted from his lack of experience in high office and his lack of self-confidence. The president was also betrayed by his trusted friends and advisers. Nevertheless, Harding was aware of his limitations and worked hard to build on his strengths. He once remarked to a reporter, "I cannot hope to be one of the greatest presidents, but perhaps I may be remembered as one of the best loved." Unfortunately, despite his efforts, he failed to become either.

TIMELINE

1865   Warren Gamaliel Harding is born in Blooming Grove, Ohio, on November 2. He is the first of eight children in his family.

1873   The Harding family moves to Caledonia, Ohio.

1875   Harding's father acquires the *Caledonia Argus* newspaper. Warren works at the paper after school. Harding learns to play the cornet.

1879   No longer able to afford their Caledonia house, the Hardings move to a small farm in a neighboring county. Harding enters Iberia College.

1880   Florence Harding marries her first husband, Pete De Wolfe.

1882   Harding graduates from Iberia College.

1884   Harding and two friends purchase the *Marion Star* newspaper.

1886   Florence Harding divorces Pete De Wolfe.

1891   Warren and Florence Harding marry. The wedding is held in a home that the couple had built for themselves.

1892   Warren G. Harding visits Washington, D.C., for the first time.

1895   In April Harding attends the Marion County Republican Convention. His work for the Republican Party helps him to become better known in the area.

1898–1903   Harding serves in the Ohio State Senate.

1904–1906   Harding serves as lieutenant governor of Ohio.

1905   Harding begins his relationship with Carrie Phillips.

1910 Harding runs for governor of Ohio and loses. Harding ends his relationship with Carrie.

1912 Harding gives the nominating speech at the Republican National Convention for President William Howard Taft's second term.

1914 Harding is elected as a U.S. senator from Ohio. World War I begins.

1917 Harding begins a relationship with Nan Britton. The United States enters World War I in April.

1918 An armistice, or peace agreement, is signed between Germany and the Allies in November, ending World War I.

1919 Former president Theodore Roosevelt dies on January 6. Harding attends the funeral, and other Republicans begin to think of him as a possible presidential candidate in the upcoming election. Nan Britton gives birth to Warren G. Harding's only child on October 22.

1920 In June Harding wins the Republican Party nomination for president of the United States. From July to September, Harding conducts his front porch campaign. On November 2, Warren G. Harding is elected twenty-ninth president of the United States.

1921 Harding's presidential inauguration is held on March 4.

1921–1922 The Washington Conference, resulting in several naval disarmament treaties, is held.

1922 Harding becomes the first president to broadcast a speech by radio.

1923 Harding's Voyage of Understanding takes place from June to August. Harding dies on August 2.

1924 Florence Harding dies on November 21.

SOURCE NOTES

7 "The Return to Normalcy President: In His Own Words," *The American President,* 2002, <www.americanpresident.org> (April 9, 2002).

8 Francis Russell, *The Shadow of Blooming Grove: Warren G. Harding in His Times* (New York: McGraw-Hill, 1968), 12.

8 Ibid.

10 Ibid., 37.

16 Charles L. Mee Jr., *The Ohio Gang: The World of Warren G. Harding* (New York: M. Evans and Co., 1981), 53.

18 Ibid., 45.

20 Ibid., 47.

20 Ibid., 49.

22 Ibid., 50.

22 Ibid.

23 Linda R. Wade, *Warren G. Harding: Twenty-ninth President of the United States* (Chicago: Children's Press, 1989), 22.

24 Russell, *The Shadow of Blooming Grove: Warren G. Harding in His Times,* 80.

25 Carl Sferrazza Anthony, *Florence Harding: The First Lady, The Jazz Age, and the Death of America's Most Scandalous President* (New York: William Morrow & Co., 1998), 3.

28 Russell, *The Shadow of Blooming Grove: Warren G. Harding in His Times,* 85.

31 "Warren G. Harding Quotes," *Friends of Harding Home and Memorial,* n.d., <www .hardingfriends.org> (April 9, 2002).

35 Russell, *The Shadow of Blooming Grove: Warren G. Harding in His Times,* 102.

36 Ibid., 104.

36 Ibid., 106.

37 Mee, *The Ohio Gang: The World of Warren G. Harding,* 59.

37 Robert K. Murray, *The Harding Era: Warren G. Harding and His Administration* (Minneapolis: University of Minnesota Press, 1969), 11.

43 "Warren G. Harding Quotes," *Friends of Harding Home and Memorial,* n.d., <www .hardingfriends.org> (April 9, 2002).

48 Murray, *The Harding Era: Warren G. Harding and His Administration,* 19.

49 Anthony, *Florence Harding: The First Lady, The Jazz Age, and the Death of America's Most Scandalous President,* 119.

51 Russell, *The Shadow of Blooming Grove: Warren G. Harding in His Times,* 264.

54 Nan Britton, *The President's Daughter* (New York: Elizabeth Ann Guild, 1927), 7.

55 Anthony, *Florence Harding: The First Lady, The Jazz Age, and the Death of America's Most Scandalous President,* 147.

56 Ibid.

57 Ibid., 148.

57 Russell, *The Shadow of Blooming Grove: Warren G. Harding in His Times,* 317.

57 Ibid., 318.

57 Ibid.

57 Ibid.

61 Murray, *The Harding Era: Warren G. Harding and His Administration,* 25.

64 Mee, *The Ohio Gang: The World of Warren G. Harding,* 80.

64 Ibid., 79.

65 Robert K. Murray, *The Politics of Normalcy: Governmental Theory and Practice in the Harding-*

Coolidge Era (New York: W. W. Norton & Co., 1973), 8.

65 Mee, *The Ohio Gang: The World of Warren G. Harding,* 85.

68 Timothy Walch, "Harding, Warren Gamaliel," *World Book Online Reference Center,* 2003, <www.worldbookonline.com/ar?/n a/ar/cp/ar245880.htm.> (August 19, 2003).

69 Ibid.

69 Murray, *The Harding Era: Warren G. Harding and His Administration,* 23.

69 Mee, *The Ohio Gang: The World of Warren G. Harding,* 92.

70 Murray, *The Harding Era: Warren G. Harding and His Administration,* 23.

70 Ibid.

71 *Atlanta Constitution,* June 13, 1920, C4.

73 "Quotations by Author; Warren G. Harding (1865–1923)" *The Quotations Page Website,* 2003, <www.quotationspage.com> (October 30, 2003).

74 Mee, *The Ohio Gang: The World of Warren G. Harding,* 104.

75 Ibid., 107.

77 Eugene P. Trani and David L. Wilson, *The Presidency of Warren G. Harding* (Lawrence: The University Press of Kansas, 1977), 26.

78 Murray, *The Harding Era: Warren G. Harding and His Administration,* 53.

78 Ibid.

80 Russell, *The Shadow of Blooming Grove: Warren G. Harding in His Times,* 414.

81 Mee, *The Ohio Gang: The World of Warren G. Harding,* 107.

83 Trani and Wilson, *The Presidency of Warren G. Harding,* 182.

83 Stoddard, Henry L., *It Costs to Be President.* (New York: Harper & Brothers, 1938), 22.

83 Anthony, *Florence Harding: The First Lady, The Jazz Age, and the Death of America's Most Scandalous President,* 238.

84 Mee, *The Ohio Gang: The World of Warren G. Harding,* 115.

88 Trani and Wilson, *The Presidency of Warren G. Harding,* 38.

88 Ibid.

90 Robert H. Ferrell, *The Strange Deaths of President Harding* (Columbia: University of Missouri Press, 1996), 116.

93 Murray, *The Harding Era: Warren G. Harding and His Administration,* 447.

93 Mee, *The Ohio Gang: The World of Warren G. Harding,* 215.

95 Murray, *The Harding Era: Warren G. Harding and His Administration,* 445.

96 Mee, *The Ohio Gang: The World of Warren G. Harding,* 217.

96 Ibid., 218.

97 Ibid., 219.

97 Ibid., 220.

98 Wade, *Warren G. Harding: Twenty-ninth President of the United States,* 84.

103 Murray, *The Harding Era: Warren G. Harding and His Administration,* 123.

SELECTED BIBLIOGRAPHY

Adams, Samuel Hopkins. *Incredible Era: The Life and Times of Warren Gamaliel Harding.* Boston: Houghton Mifflin, 1939.

Anthony, Carl Sferrazza. *Florence Harding: The First Lady, The Jazz Age, and The Death of America's Most Scandalous President.* New York: William Morrow & Co., 1998.

Britton, Nan. *The President's Daughter.* New York: Elizabeth Ann Guild, 1927.

Daugherty, Harry M. *The Inside Story of the Harding Tragedy.* Freeport, NY: Books for Libraries Press, 1932.

Ferrell, Robert H. *The Strange Deaths of President Harding.* Columbia: University of Missouri Press, 1996.

Mee, Charles L., Jr. *The Ohio Gang: The World of Warren G. Harding.* New York: M. Evans and Co., 1981.

Moran, Philip. *Warren Harding.* Dobbs Ferry, NY: Oceana Publications, 1970.

Murray, Robert K. *The Harding Era: Warren G. Harding and His Administration.* Minneapolis: University of Minnesota Press, 1969.

————. *The Politics of Normalcy: Governmental Theory and Practice in the Harding-Coolidge Era.* New York: W. W. Norton & Co., 1973.

Pusey, Merlo J. *Charles Evans Hughes.* Vol. 1. New York: Macmillan, 1957.

Russell, Francis. *The Shadow of Blooming Grove: Warren G. Harding in His Times.* New York: McGraw-Hill, 1968.

Sinclair, Andrew. *The Available Man: Warren Gamaliel Harding.* New York: Macmillan, 1965.

Stoddard, Henry L. *It Costs to Be President.* New York: Harper & Brothers, 1938.

Trani, Eugene P., and David L. Wilson. *The Presidency of Warren G. Harding.* Lawrence: The University Press of Kansas, 1977.

Further Reading and Websites

Allen, Michael Geoffrey. *Calvin Coolidge.* Berkeley Heights, NJ: Enslow Publishers, 2002.

Canadeo, Anne. *Warren G. Harding, 29th President of the United States.* Ada, OK: Garrett Educational Corp., 1990.

Cleveland, Will, and Mark Alvarez. *Yo, Millard Fillmore! (And All Those Other Presidents You Don't Know).* Brookfield, CT: Millbrook Press, 1997.

Dommermuth-Costa, Carol. *Woodrow Wilson.* Minneapolis, MN: Lerner Publications Company, 2003.

Feinberg, Barbara Silberdick. *America's First Ladies: Changing Expectations.* Danbury, CT: Franklin Watts, 1998.

"Florence Kling Harding." *The White House.* <www.whitehouse.gov/history/firstladies/fh29.html>. Read about this capable First Lady who stood behind her husband and assisted him in his endeavors.

"Inaugural Address of Warren G. Harding." *The Avalon Project at Yale Law School.* <www.yale.edu/lawweb/avalon/president/inaug/harding.htm>. This site provides the text of the speech given by Harding on his inauguration, March 4, 1921.

Kronwetter, Michael. *Political Parties of the United States.* Berkeley Heights, NJ: Enslow Publishers, 1996.

Krull, Kathleen. *Lives of the Presidents: Fame, Shame, and What the Neighbors Thought.* San Diego: Harcourt, 1998.

Morin, Isobel V. *Politics American Style: Political Parties in American History.* Brookfield, CT: Millbrook Press, 1999.

Thorndike, Jonathan L. *The Teapot Dome Scandal Trial: A Headline Court Case.* Berkeley Heights, NJ: Enslow Publishers, 2001.

Wade, Linda R. *Warren G. Harding: Twenty-ninth President of the United States.* Chicago: Children's Press, 1989.

"Warren G. Harding." *The White House.* <www.whitehouse.gov/history/presidents/wh29.html>. The official White House website includes biographies of all the presidents, including Harding.

INDEX

ABOUT THE AUTHOR

Award-winning children's book author Elaine Landau worked as a newspaper reporter, a children's book editor, and a youth services librarian before becoming a full-time writer. She has written more than two hundred nonfiction books for young readers. Landau has a bachelor's degree in English and journalism from New York University and a master's degree in library and information science from Pratt Institute. She lives in Miami, Florida, with her husband, Norman, and their son, Michael. You can visit Elaine Landau at her website, www.elainelandau.com.

———————————— ◇ ————————————

PHOTO ACKNOWLEDGMENTS